MW00813277

99 EPIC

THINGS TO DO

ST. AUGUSTINE, FL

Make your trip epic!

99EPIC 📷 | ✈ | 🍴

Although the author and publisher have made every effort to ensure that the
information in this book was correct at press time, the author and publisher do not
assume and hereby disclaim any liability to any party for any loss, damage, or disruption caused
by errors or omissions, whether such errors or omissions result from negligence, accident, or any
other cause. All quotes are cited to give credit to the original author
if not cited they are either unknown or anonymous. This book is meant for your
entertainment, all recommendations and references are strictly the unsolicited
opinions of the authors.

No part of this publication may be reproduced, stored in a retrieval system, or transmitted in any
form or by any means, electronic, mechanical, photocopying, recording, or otherwise, without
written permission of the publisher.

For information regarding permission, write to:
Attention: Crown Atlantic Publishing
136 ML King Ave., St. Augustine, FL 32084

Copyright 2016 by Christina & Philip Benjamin
All rights reserved.
Published in the United States by Crown Atlantic Publishing

Printed in the United States of America
First edition hardcover printed, 2016
ISBN# 978-0-9883375-6-5

My epic adventure began on

_____

This is who joined me:

1.)_____

2.)_____

3.)_____

4.)_____

5.)_____

6.)_____

Defining EPIC

Epic: (ep-ik) – adjective
1. heroic; majestic; impressively great.
2. Slang. Spectacular; very impressive; awesome.

Our definition of EPIC:
Sometimes being "Epic" isn't about doing something extreme or over the top. It's taking a small, ordinary thing and enjoying every aspect of it. It's taking pleasure in the little things, being present and enjoying your surroundings, savoring the moment, doing good deeds, passing on positivity, making unforgettable memories and sharing them with others.

So wherever you are, go out and be  EPIC!

Find
Beauty
in the
SMALL THINGS

We believe in taking time to *enjoy life and be EPIC.*

Our EPIC Story:

Sometimes life throws challenges at us that we're not prepared for, but it's up to us to decide how we're affected. We're a couple who has chosen to follow a path of love, life and adventure. We try to see beauty in everything and let each life encounter change us for the better. We believe in leaving the places we visit better than we found them and allowing them to influence us in a way that we can carry with us always.

You only have one life, live an EPIC one!

VISIT US ONLINE
www.99epic.com

SHARE YOUR EPIC ADVENTURES WITH US

FACEBOOK.COM/99EPIC   TWITTER.COM/99EPIC_TRAVEL   INSTAGRAM.COM/99EPIC

OUR EPIC LOCATION:

Each destination we chose for our EPIC series has special meaning, but maybe none so special as St. Augustine, FL. We chose St. Augustine as the first location in the EPIC series for many reasons. It's really where it ALL started. This town has housed us through college, friendships and family. It's the oldest continually occupied town in the nation, and we're now blessed enough to call it home. We've made so many amazing memories here and can't wait to share them with you.

Use the pages of this book to capture your own EPIC memories of St. Augustine that you'll be able to revisit for years to come.

Throughout this book we'll share some major highlights not to be missed in St. Augustine as well as some of our local favorites that you won't find on the typical tourist map.

Are you ready? Your EPIC adventure awaits.

Disclaimer: This is not your typical tour book, rather an inspirational way to view a location that will leave an EPIC impression on your heart. We were not endorsed by or obligated to recommend any of the locations, quotes or activities mentioned in this book.

ST. AUGUSTINE

"Each day holds the possibilities for great discoveries and hidden joy..." – Stephanie Ackerman

Fort Castillo de San Marcos is an excellent place to start your St. Augustine adventure. It's the oldest masonry fort in the continental United States, with construction beginning in 1672. Possession of the fort has changed six times, and it has served as a military prison. It's a great place to catch the sunrise and watch dolphin playing in the bay.

Sunrise.

"Each morning we are born again. What we do today is what matters most." - Buddha

One of the best places to view the sunrise is from the bayfront sea wall. After you enjoy the view, take an early jog or walk through town before the day starts to enjoy the quiet beauty.

#3 EAT

"Country Cookin' warms the heart & soothes the soul."

Creekside Dinery

This truly hidden gem is nestled among beautiful magnolia trees on Gonzalez Creek. Open since 1991, this eatery knows how to serve southern style seafood like no one else in town. They're famous for their plank fish and creekside shrimp. Dine outdoors under the canopy of live oaks and white lights while listening to live music. You can even roast marshmallows over the fire pit for dessert.

ONE-OF-A-KIND
HIDDEN
GEM ST. AUGUSTINE FLORIDA
99EPIC

"Not all who wander are lost." – J. R. R. Tolkien

St. George Street, one of the oldest in the nation, is a wonderful place to wander. It starts at the city gates and houses the "oldest school house." You'll find a vast array of shops, taverns, musicians and history here. If you visit early in the morning or late at night you can get some beautiful photos of the deserted street. It's fun to imagine what it might have been like all those years ago to stroll the cobblestone.

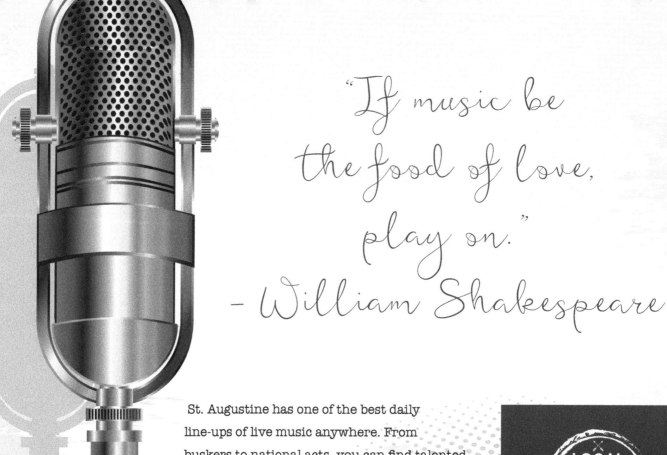

"If music be
the food of love,
play on."
– William Shakespeare

St. Augustine has one of the best daily line-ups of live music anywhere. From buskers to national acts, you can find talented musicians playing all over town. Listening to live music is a great way to immerse yourself into the folky beach vibe of this town. Loosen your inhibitions and sing along.

LOCAL TIP

OC White's, Mi Casa, No Name, Sangrias and Café 11 are some of our favs for local live music.

ADVENTURE: NOUN | AD-VEN-TURE |
An exciting or dangerous experience.

Take a SUP Lesson. Stand Up Paddle Boards are a fun way to explore the first coast. Let's Go Stand Up offers great lessons and tours for all ages.

"Great is the fortune of he who possesses a good bottle, a good book, a good friend."
– Moliere

No trip to St. Augustine is complete without a visit to the San Sebastian Winery. Take the free tour and sample their wines. Grab a bottle to enjoy back at your B&B or just ask for some at the local restaurants who happily carry the popular vino.

 LOCAL TIP

While at the Winery, head up to the rooftop wine bar at sunset to catch some great live music and enjoy your wine.

"Kind words can be short and easy to speak, but their echoes are truly endless."
– Mother Teresa

There are over a dozen historic churches in St. Augustine. Visit one, light a candle, say a prayer, or make a donation. Flagler Memorial Presbyterian Church is absolutely stunning. Henry Flagler erected this church as a memorial for his late daughter, Jenny Louise. You can tour it during the week.

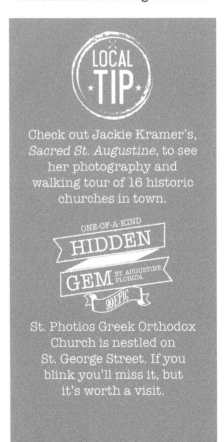

LOCAL TIP

Check out Jackie Kramer's, *Sacred St. Augustine*, to see her photography and walking tour of 16 historic churches in town.

ONE-OF-A-KIND
HIDDEN
GEM ST. AUGUSTINE FLORIDA
99EPIC

St. Photios Greek Orthodox Church is nestled on St. George Street. If you blink you'll miss it, but it's worth a visit.

> *"Love is composed of a single soul inhabiting two bodies."*
> *- Aristotle*

Visit A Love Tree

A love tree is two trees growing together as one. The phenomenon of a love tree is that they can't be separated, spawning the legend that if you kiss your true love underneath the love tree, you will be together for eternity.

"I've been through the desert on a horse with no name…"
– AMERICA

The lyrics may be a little different, but the Bar with No Name is just as memorable as the famous song. It has one of the best views in town. Enjoy live music and libations at this local late night watering hole, while pondering what name you'd give the Bar with No Name.

LOCAL TIP

Relax here at sunset and watch the beautiful orange colors of the sun bounce off of the Castillo de San Marcos.

"Smell the sea and feel the sky. Let your soul and spirit fly." – Van Morrison

ST. AUGUSTINE BEACH

With nearly 2 miles of pristine white sand beaches to enjoy, St. Augustine Beach offers something for everyone. You can hike on Anastasia State Park, fish from the pier, catch a wave, enjoy a meal, take a drive, ride your bike or just enjoy the view.

"If you have good thoughts they will shine out of your face like sunbeams and you will always look lovely."
– Roald Dahl

Meditation is a great way to get in tune with yourself and the new place you're visiting. Center yourself and look deep within. Are you in need of peace, relaxation, adventure, love, or creativity? Find what your soul is craving and seek it out in your EPIC adventure.

"I regard the theater as the greatest of all art forms. The most immediate way a human being can share with another the sense of what it is to be a human being."
— Oscar Wilde

LIMELIGHT

The Limelight Theater has been delivering theatrical entertainment to St. Augustine patrons for the past 25 years. It's a great place to catch a local theater show. They also offer educational courses and open casting calls.

"The best wines are those you drink with friends."

Monk's Vineyard is a hidden gem. This St. George Street staple has a special place in our hearts. It's been owned and operated by the charismatic Hank Williams for as long as we can remember. Whether you go in with a group or on your own, Hank is always happy to entertain. He's seen St. Augustine grow and change and we always love talking to him about it. He makes the best sangria in town and also serves some pretty rare and eclectic bottles of wine and craft beverages. His hours are as assorted as his spirits, but it's worth fitting Monk's into your visit. Ask him to sign this page and send us a pic. A stop at Monk's will be something you'll never forget.

" *Monks Vineyard is a portal to the past and future.*" – Hank Williams

LOCAL TIP Buy a beverage and sit on his front patio and watch the world go by.

"Explore. Dream. Discover."
– Mark Twain

There is so much to see and do in St. Augustine. One of the best ways to explore the city is through a historic Trolley Tour. Learn the lay of the land and soak up some history.

Check out these two trolley companies in town.
Old Town Trolley Tours & Ripley's Red Trains

LOCAL TIP This is something we love to do on our first day in any new city. You get some great facts, a handy map and can plan where you want to go next.

There's so much beauty in St. Augustine. Take a moment and let it seep in. Let the wonders of this historic town inspire you. Sketch something you see or feel.

"Laughter is timeless, imagination has no age, and dreams are forever." — Walt Disney

Crave

Craving something delicious? Check out Crave Food Truck. This local gem serves up fierce, fresh lunch - food truck style. Run by Andres Gaurdiola and Renee Spadaro, Crave embodies the shop local vibe of St. Augustine. They use local produce and resources and always give you service with a smile. With outdoor seating and a view of San Sebastian river, you can't go wrong at Crave.

ONE-OF-A-KIND
HIDDEN
GEM ST. AUGUSTINE FLORIDA
99EPIC

"We are extremely passionate about not only healthy living but sharing this passion with as many people as we can. We seek out and choose the freshest, locally sourced ingredients because we feel strongly about supporting local farmers as well as ensuring the highest quality products are being used."
–Andres Gaurdiola

LOCAL TIP

The wraps and smoothies are out of this world. Our fav is the Tuna Wrap.

"It is a *happy talent* to know how to *play*."
– Ralph Waldo Emerson

MINI GOLF ON THE BAYFRONT

There's a plethora of great mini-golf courses in St. Augustine, but there's just something nostalgic about putting on the greens that overlook the grand bayfront. Imagine early settlers strutting along the promenade in the 1800s as you play the course. It's not hard to do with the clip clop of horse drawn carriages as your background music.

"Be silly. You're allowed to be silly. There's nothing wrong with it."
— Jimmy Fallon

Check out a local thrift store while you're in town. St. Augustine has some amazing second hand stores. Travel back in time as you tour the racks. You might find a blast from the past that you just can't live without. JUST FOR FUN: If you are traveling with friends each pick out something the other has to wear for the rest of the day. Check out The Closet on Cordova Street and Cool & Collected on San Marco Ave for some good thrift store finds.

"In every walk with nature, one receives far more than he seeks." — John Muir

Anastasia State Park

You can hike, swim, beachcomb, bird watch, camp and explore the 1600 acre park. There's even concessions and bike, boat and board rentals on site. This is a great place to escape to your own quiet slice of St. Augustine paradise.

"Art is not what you see, but what you make others see."
– Edgar Degas

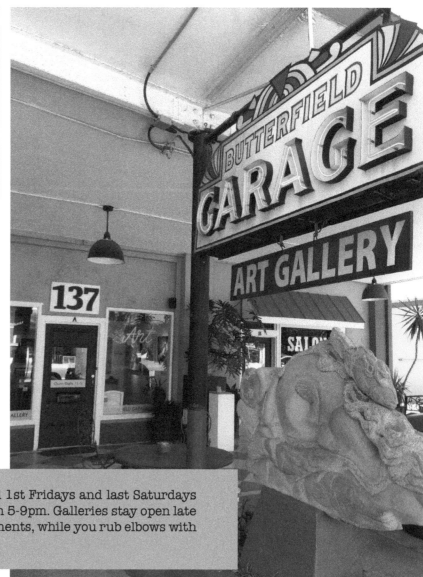

Art Galleries are abundant in St. Augustine. The town's history has always been rich in culture, music and art. There are over 30 galleries nestled among the winding streets. Avilés and King Street are an artist's dream, littered with galleries galore. Even Flagler College has a gallery to exhibit pieces by students.

JUST FOR FUN: Stare at a piece of art and ponder its meaning.

LOCAL TIP

Art Walks are held 1st Fridays and last Saturdays of each month from 5-9pm. Galleries stay open late and serve refreshments, while you rub elbows with local artists.

"At the beach life is different... Time doesn't move hour to hour but mood to moment. We live by the currents, plan by the tides and follow the sun." — Sandy Gingras

"A" STREET ON ST. AUGUSTINE BEACH

This is where you'll find the local surfers hanging out. You can rent boards or pick up wax at The Pit Surf Shop. Don't forget to grab a bite to eat after your surf sesh at Beachcomber or Stir It Up.

LOCAL TIP

Beachcomber has one of the best beach front dining locations nestled in the dunes.

"FIRST WE EAT, THEN WE DO EVERYTHING ELSE."
— M. F. K. FISHER

Mango Mango's is a local beach fav. Their Floribbean Fusion menu is like no other. Yuka fries, corn cakes, tropical drinks and the music to match will make you think you're in the Caribbean Islands.

LOCAL TIP

Try Mango Mango's famous Corn Cakes. They are not to be missed.

"Those who do not remember the past are condemned to repeat it."
— George Santayana

OLD JAIL

The Old Jail probably has some of the coolest and spookiest history in town. Go on a tour to see first hand what prison life was like in the tiny cells. Get some great facts and photo ops along the way.

Watch the Sunset. St. Augustine has some of the most beautiful sunsets we've ever seen. Grab a good book and a glass of wine and unwind as you watch the sunset.

"I long for the solitude of a sunset at sea, and the chill of the breeze coming in with the eve. For the motion of my boat, as she swings on her rode, and the beauty of the stars, in the evenings last glow."

— R. C. Gibbons.

LOCAL TIP

A great place to watch the sunset is at Beaches restaurant in Vilano where you can enjoy a meal in the sand while watching the sunset over the intercostal.

"**You can find me where the *music* meets *the ocean*.**"

Music at the Pier is a free concert series that runs from May - October every Wednesday from 6-9pm. You can pack a cooler, beach chairs and your favorite beverages. Hang out in the sand while local bands showcase their talents in the pier pavilion. A different local restaurant is featured each week, cooking up great fare for your enjoyment.

LOCAL TIP

Go early to beat the crowds. This is a great family event, kid and pet friendly.

"FEED YOUR SOUL."

Mojo's BBQ is a favorite for locals and tourists alike. They do BBQ right and stock their bar pretty well too. You won't find a better selection of whiskey anywhere in town. You can even get a flight to try out a few new ones.

LOCAL TIP

The smoked turkey and mac & cheese is to die for.

"Whatever good things we build end up building us."
— Jim Rohn

The Bridge of Lions is the iconic showpiece of downtown St. Augustine. The pair of Medici marble lions have guarded the city since 1927. Stop by for a photo op.

JUST FOR FUN: Stump people with this trivia – What are the names of the two original lions at the bridge?

Answer: Firm and Faithful.

" *Dance is a way to lose yourself and find yourself… all at the same time.* "

With so many great places to listen to music in St. Augustine, dancing is an everyday event here. Cut a rug at A1A Aleworks or Mi Casa while you listen to some awesome live music.

"Shells sink, dreams float. Life is good, on our boat." - Jimmy Buffet

One of the best ways to see St. Augustine is by boat. Rent a pontoon boat and explore the first coast.

LOCAL TIP

Beach at a tidal sandbar and enjoy your own private island all throughout the intracoastal. Pack a picnic and enjoy a day on the water.

"One cannot **think well, love well, sleep well,** if one has not dined well."

– Virginia Woolf

In our opinion, The Floridian is probably one of the best restaurants in town. Their success is evident, as they've expanded to a larger space. The Florida vibe is alive in all the fresh local dishes they serve. The creative menu changes seasonally to support the farm-to-table style of this restaurant.

LOCAL TIP

Try the local catch on a farm fresh salad and for dessert, don't miss the cupcakes, they are divine.

The Floridian

"Alcohol:
Because no great story ever started with someone eating a salad."

The St. Augustine Distillery is a newer addition to town. Check out the free daily tours where you can learn the history of how the distillery came about, tour the plant and sample some refreshing spirits.

LOCAL TIP

Don't miss a chance to enjoy a gourmet meal and handcrafted cocktail at the adjoining Ice Plant restaurant. The ambience will transport you to a bygone era and have you humming jazz tunes while you sip out of a copper mug.

Namaste:

(nah-mas-tay)

(n.) My soul honors your soul. I honor the place in you where the entire universe resides. I honor the light, love, truth, beauty and peace within you, because it is also within me. In sharing these things we are united, we are the same, we are one.

After a long day of exploring unwind with some ____ Go love your ____

LOCAL TIP

8 Limbs Yoga offers great classes or do it on your own at the beach or on the deck by the Bridge of Lions.

"THE OCEAN STIRS THE HEART, INSPIRES THE IMAGINATION AND BRINGS ETERNAL JOY TO THE SOUL." - WYLAND

OCEAN HAMMOCK PARK

If you're looking for a secluded spot to get some fresh air, check out Ocean Hammock Park. The wooded boardwalk leads you through wildlife, wetlands and dunes. You'll get to enjoy St. Augustine beach in a natural state.

"Live a spicy life."

LOCAL TIP

Order the famous 1905 Salad and a pitcher of Sangria.

Columbia restaurant is a culinary landmark in St. Augustine. Dining in the three story Columbian casa is a must. Even on the busiest days you can always get a seat in this massive restaurant.

"If you want to find happiness set yourself free from the ghosts of your past." —Nishan Panwar

Ghost Tours are a terrific way to explore St. Augustine and learn its tumultuous history. There are many different options available in town, from walking tours or trolley tours to private hearse rides.

TROLLEY OF THE DOOMED

LOCAL TIP

Go at night to add to the spook factor. Sheriff Doug's walking tour is one of our favorites.

"*Life is a song, sing it.*"

JUST FOR FUN:

Sing along with a street performer, musician, or by yourself. It's so freeing. Write down what tunes you sing to while in town.

_____

_____

_____

_____

_____

"Life is better with a little sand between your toes."

Beaches at Vilano is one of our favorite places to dine waterfront. Your toes are actually in the sand here. You can even boat to Beaches. This tropical bar gives you that island feel complete with tiki bar, beach vibe and Caribbean music. It's a local favorite for sure.

LOCAL TIP

Try the Sunset Shrimp Tacos with tots and a bucket of beer. It doesn't get much better.

"OH WITCHING AND SWEET IS THE MUSIC EARTH STEALS FROM IRON SHOD FEET."
— WILL H. OGILVIE

//

One of the best ways to see the town is by horse and carriage. These guided tours give you the authentic feel of old town St. Augustine and can be tailored for any occasion. Enjoy the scenery while your driver narrates. There are even horse drawn food & wine tours for large groups.

LOCAL TIP

Grab a carriage at the bayfront and pack a snack and a drink for the ride through town.

"Aye, tales there be plenty in this cursed place."
– Pirates of the Caribbean

Pirating was and still is a popular past time in this coastal town. St. Augustine was burned to the ground twice by pirate raids. Check out the Pirate Museum to learn all about the rich history of Pirates in St. Augustine. Tour the El Galleon Spanish tall ship if it's in port or take a ride on the Black Raven Pirate Ship. If you happen to visit in November you can even catch the annual Pirate Gathering, when the streets are flooded by the most authentic bunch of scurvy riddled scoundrels you've ever seen.

LOCAL TIP

If you want to look the part during your pirating check out The Pirate Store in the St. George Street shops.

Yum!
"Tacos + Beach = Perfection"

The Taco Shop

The Taco Shop is home to the legendary UFO taco. People flock from all over to try the giant tortilla creation. There are two locations, but the island atmosphere of the beachside Taco Shop on A1A is tough to beat. You can show up in your swimsuit and flip-flops. Even Fido is welcome.

Most Talked About Taco:
The UFO

Nalu's

Nalu's Tropical Takeout is the godfather of the St. Augustine taco empire. This food truck has been serving up tropical eats before food trucks were hip. A favorite among surfers, this eatery is known for delicious tacos made with simple, fresh, healthy ingredients and a bit of Hawaiian flavor – paying homage to the owner's fond memories of the North Shore.

Must Have Meal:
Mermaid Wrap

Mojo's Tacos

Mojo's Tacos offers endless possibilities with its "build-your-own" style menu. Create the taco, burrito or salad of your dreams with a wide variety of fresh and unique ingredients like fish, shrimp, tofu and tempeh.

Most Talked About Taco:
The Double Decker

PLAY

"Some days are simply meant for playing."
– Mary Anne Radmacher

Play in the surf like you're a kid again.
Splash and be free.

"MUSIC IS A MORTAL LAW. IT GIVES SOUL TO THE UNIVERSE. WINGS TO THE MIND. FLIGHT AND CHARM AND GAIETY TO LIFE AND TO EVERYTHING." — PLATO

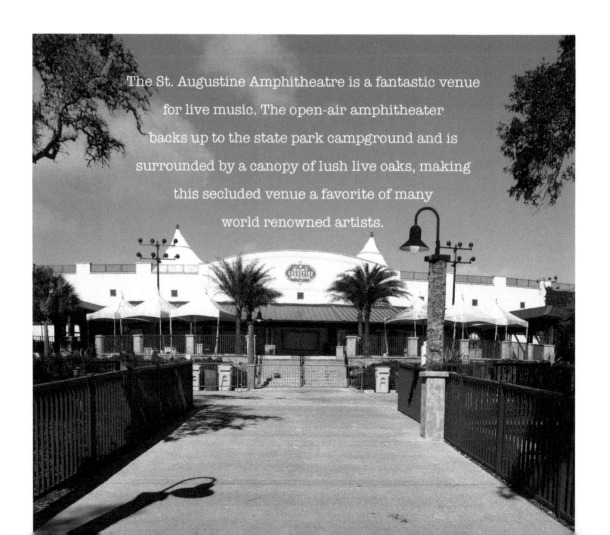

The St. Augustine Amphitheatre is a fantastic venue for live music. The open-air amphitheater backs up to the state park campground and is surrounded by a canopy of lush live oaks, making this secluded venue a favorite of many world renowned artists.

"There's nothing more exciting than meeting new people, hearing their stories and being inspired."

Talk to a local. This is something you can do wherever your travels may take you. There's no better way to find out what new events are going on or where local hangouts are than to talk to someone from the place you're visiting. Plus, you never know where your connection will lead.

MEET A LOCAL

ANTIQUES

"THE THRILL OF THE HUNT, FOR MAYBE TODAY, I WILL FIND A TREASURE FROM MANY YESTERDAYS."

Go antiquing in the uptown shopping district. It's amazing what nostalgic memories you'll discover in a town with history this rich.

"Seas the day."

FIND A GREAT SPOT IN THE SEAFARING TOWN TO SIT BACK,
RELAX AND WATCH THE BOATS COME AND GO.

"When in Rome..."

Many restaurants in town serve fresh, locally caught seafood. It goes right from the boat to the belly so to speak. Tuna, Mahi, Flounder, Grouper, or Snapper are always a sure bet for some great local eats.

LOCAL TIP

Catch 27 is an amazing little seafood joint on Charlotte St. where they make all their menu items with the catch of the day.

AVILÉS STREET

Wanderlust (n.): a strong desire for or impulse to wander or travel and explore the world.

Avilés Street is tucked away from the busy hustle and bustle of the group tours. It offers small shops, art galleries and some excellent European street style dining.

"Life is like riding a **bicycle.** *To keep your balance you must* **keep moving."**
- Albert Einstein

A great way to cover ground and discover all St. Augustine has to offer is to rent bicycles.

LOCAL TIP

Ride through the residential areas and look at all the eclectic old houses. Marine, Bridge, Saragossa, Charlotte and Sevilla streets offer some beautiful historic sites.

"The desire to create is one of the deepest yearnings of the human soul." – Deiter F. Uchtdorf

Create your own artist street rubbing. It'll be a fun keepsake you can hang on to.

FUN (N.):
ENJOYMENT,
AMUSEMENT OR
LIGHT-HEARTED
PLEASURE.

PHOTO HUNT

If you think you've gotten the lay
of the land take our photo hunt
challenge. Can you find the spot
where we took this picture?
Take your own and share
it with us.

"THE WAVES OF THE SEA HELP ME GET BACK TO ME."

Vilano Beach has much to offer; boating, beaches, restaurants and parks.

LOCAL TIP

During the week this beach is pretty quiet. You can drive on and walk in the peaceful surf.

VILANO BEACH

GIVE BACK

"We make a living by what we get, but we make a life by what we give."
– Winston Churchill

There's something symbiotic about giving back to a place that gives you happy memories. We try to pay it forward everywhere we go. If you're looking for a way to give back in St. Augustine, donate to the St. Francis House, a shelter for the homeless, on Washington Street.

"FOR ME THE CINEMA IS NOT A SLICE OF LIFE, BUT A PIECE OF CAKE."
- Alfred Hitchcock

The Corazon Cinema & Café is a unique experience, where you can enjoy dinner and a movie all at once. You'll find unique indie films, documentaries and cult classics here. There's a full menu, with beer and wine and an elegant theater room to enjoy your meal and show. Great for a rainy day or if you just want to avoid the crowds.

WINE

> "Wine is constant proof that god loves us and loves to see us happy." — Benjamin Franklin

Unwind with a glass of wine at The Gifted Cork or Carrera Wine Cellar while you're in town. Both have extensive wine collections and friendly, knowledgeable staff. Check out The Gifted Cork if you want to stop in for a quick tasting at a great price, plus you get a souvenir glass. Stop by Carrera Wine Cellar to create your own wine flight, sample wines by the ounce or just relax, listen to some live music or play a board game.

"GET SOME VITAMIN SEA."

Collect seashells on the beach.

This childhood activity never gets old. Just enjoy the moment.

"Man cannot discover new oceans unless he has the courage to lose sight of the shore." —Andre Gide

There are so many great ways to see all that St. Augustine has to offer. One of our favorites is by sea. Take a sightseeing cruise around the first coast and encounter the beautiful sea life. Dolphin, sea turtles, manatee and a variety of birds frequently grace St. Augustine's water tours.

LOCAL TIP

Check out The Victory III and Schooner Freedom Charters. They run multiple cruises each day.

WHEREVER YOU GO, NO MATTER WHAT THE WEATHER, ALWAYS BRING YOUR OWN SUNSHINE."

– Anthony J. D'Angelo

One of the best things about St. Augustine is the weather. The coastal north Florida town experiences some of the most beautiful weather in the state, with a steady sea breeze and seasonal weather patterns.

LOCAL TIP

October is a great time of year. Avg temps: high 83, low 61.

83° 61°

> " Given enough *coffee,* one could rule the world. "

Frequent coffee breaks are crucial to seeing it all in St. Augustine. Luckily there are an abundance of local coffee houses in town. Check out this list of great spots to recharge.

LOCAL TIP

Crucial Coffee is one of our favorites. From the unique menu to the adorable English-shire feel, you'll think you stepped into Hagrid's Hut while ordering your favorite brew.

City Coffee

City Perk

Crucial Coffee

Dolce Café

DOS Coffee

Hot Shots

Juniper Market

Kookaburra

"FISHING IS NOT AN ESCAPE FROM LIFE, BUT OFTEN A DEEPER IMMERSION INTO IT."
— Harry Middleton

St. Augustine is a great place to do some fishing. Whether on a
dock at the bay, a chartered boat or with your feet in the surf, there are
plenty of options for the fishing enthusiast or novice.

#61 UNWIND

UNWIND: (v.): undo or be undone after winding or being wound.

"The bed and breakfast inn was born of sharing food with friends."

Casa de Solana

Stay at a B&B. With over 30 Bed & Breakfasts in St. Augustine, you'll surely find one that you'll enjoy. The bayfront B&B's offer amazing views or try a option closer to downtown, amid the action. One of our favorites is Casa de Solana on Avilés Street.

LOCAL TIP

If you're in town in December see if you can catch the B&B holiday tour, where you can visit them open house style.

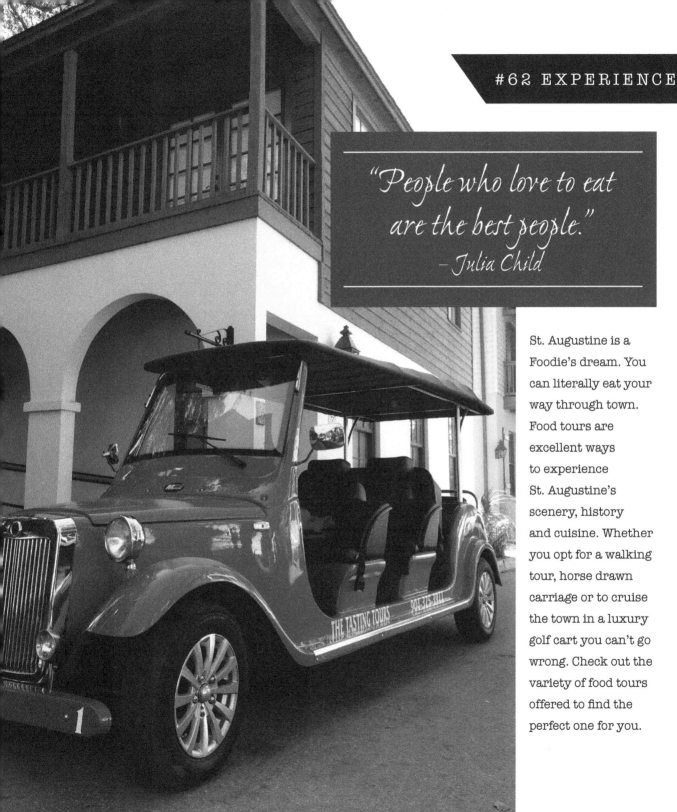

> *"People who love to eat are the best people."*
> – Julia Child

St. Augustine is a Foodie's dream. You can literally eat your way through town. Food tours are excellent ways to experience St. Augustine's scenery, history and cuisine. Whether you opt for a walking tour, horse drawn carriage or to cruise the town in a luxury golf cart you can't go wrong. Check out the variety of food tours offered to find the perfect one for you.

- PAY IT FORWARD -

"We rise by lifting others."

- Robert Ingersoll

Think of the last time you felt kismet working in your favor. Find a way to add good karma into the universe while in town. It goes a long way, especially while traveling.

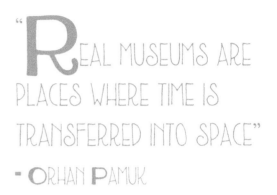

"**R**EAL MUSEUMS ARE PLACES WHERE TIME IS TRANSFERRED INTO SPACE"

- ORHAN PAMUK

The Lightner Museum, formerly Hotel Alcazar, now houses an impressive collection ranging from mummies to Tiffany glass.

LOCAL TIP

Don't miss a chance to dine at Café Alcazar. This adorable bistro is so secluded, it's actually nestled inside the original indoor swimming pool of the Hotel Alcazar. After lunch, stroll through the stunning courtyard gardens and grab a photo on the coy pond bridge.

"*DEEP IN THEIR ROOTS ALL FLOWERS KEEP THE LIGHT.*"
— *THEODORE ROETHKE*

Press a flower between these pages as a fun memento of your visit to St. Augustine.

"A DAY WITHOUT LAUGHTER IS A DAY WASTED."
— CHARLIE CHAPLIN

Ride the carousel in Davenport Park on San Marco Avenue and laugh as the world whirls around.

"A reader lives a thousand lives before he dies. The man who never reads lives only one."
– George R. R. Martin

"Come browse the book shop with heart - in the heart of St. Augustine."

Susan Von Spreckelsen & Evelyn Young (owners)

Second Reads Book Store on Cordova is a great place to discover your next great read. This local shop sells popular second hand books, hard to find special editions, children's books and even signed books from the talented local authors of St. Augustine.

LOCAL TIP

Stop here to get a book for the beach.

DARE TO BE DIFFERENT

If you want somewhere fun and different, look no further than Planet Sarbez. This eclectic bar serves killer grilled cheese, beer and wine and has an assortment of games, including an indoor shuffleboard table.

"You can't buy happiness but you can buy local and that's sort of the same thing."

Shop where the locals do at the Farmers Markets. There's one every Wednesday at the pier and every Saturday at the Amphitheater.

LOCAL TIP

Hit up local Farmers Markets when you travel so you can put together a picnic and sample the local flavor.

Beautiful streets of Lincolnville.

"We are not the makers of **history**. We are made by **history**."

– *Dr. Martin Luther King Jr.*

If you get a chance, take a trip through Historic Lincolnville. Dr. Martin Luther King's influences during the Civil Rights movement are prevalent here. You can visit historic sites on the Freedom Trail and read about the history on the plaques.

LOCAL TIP

Stop for breakfast at the Blue Hen.

ONE-OF-A-KIND
HIDDEN
GEM ST. AUGUSTINE FLORIDA
99EPIC

"Helping others is like helping yourself."
– Henry Flagler

Tour Flagler College while in St. Augustine. Henry Flagler's Ponce de Leon Hotel built in 1888 is an architectural marvel. The gorgeous 19 acre campus situated in the center of St. Augustine is one of the most beautiful in the nation.

LOCAL TIP

Check out the Tiffany stained glass windows that adorn the rotunda, now used as the student dining hall and walk through the opulent lobby to get a feel for what the hotel must have been like in its heyday.

Sangria
CAPITAL OF THE U.S.

"Take your vitamins, drink Sangria."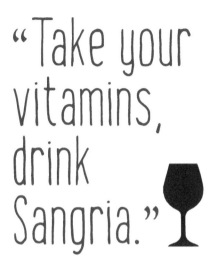

We've dubbed St. Augustine as the unofficial Sangria Capital of the U.S. Just about every watering hole in town offers their own concoction of the fruity drink, hinting to the town's Spanish influences.

LOCAL TIP

A great place to sample an array of the refreshing beverage is at Sangria's Wine & Tapas Bar on St. George Street. Try to score a table on the balcony to sip your Sangria. Don't rush, enjoy the moment and watch the bustle below you.

"Keep your wishes close to your heart and watch what happens."
– Tony DeLiso

ONE-OF-A-KIND
HIDDEN
GEM ST. AUGUSTINE FLORIDA
99EPIC

The Caños de San Francisco fountain is tucked away in a tranquil grove near the Visitor Center. It's a replica of a 16th century fountain in St. Augustine's sister city, Avilés, Spain. Visit this hidden gem while in town and make a wish.

"Nothing brings to life a forgotten memory like fragrance."
— *Christopher Poindexter*

Bath Junkie is a local shop on Hypolita Street where you can create your own fragrance and add it to spa products, like shea butter or sugar scrub. It's a fun experience to create a scent that you can take back with you. Wear the scent the whole trip, and it will cement the memory in your heart forever.

"Everyone's life could use a little dash of sea salt."

Salt Life on St. Augustine Beach is a great place to eat. You can enjoy beach views, sea breeze, indoor/outdoor dining and live music. There's even valet parking! All you have to do is sit back and relax.

LOCAL TIP

When the weather is nice, not much beats sitting on the upper deck watching a sports game with a drink in hand and the beach as your backdrop.

Festival / (n.): a day or period of
celebration

St. Francis Field plays host to the year round schedule of
festivals and fairs that bring visitors to St. Augustine.
Check out its website for a list of up coming festivals.

"Life is a journey, enjoy the ride."

Rent a scooter and cruise the town. Exploring new places in the open air capacity that scooters offer is one of the best ways to see everything. Plus, you'll find it much easier to find parking than with a car.

"The world is a book and those that do not travel read only one page."

Tour the Visitor Center on San Marco Avenue when you first get to town. Take advantage of the knowledgeable staff – they can answer questions, recommend places to visit and dine, plus they offer free maps. The Visitor Center houses interesting exhibits and a gift shop with unique local trinkets.

LOCAL TIP

Walk the grounds to visit the hidden coquina ball. It's Mile Marker Zero for the Old Spanish Trail which connected St. Augustine, FL to San Diego, CA.

"Poetry is language at its most distilled and powerful." – Rita Dove

Write a poem about what you've seen during your visit or something that

St. Augustine has inspired within you.

"SOMETIMES ALL IT TAKES IS ONE PRAYER TO CHANGE EVERYTHING."

Go to Philanthropy on King Street. The motto there is "fashion and compassion." This unique company finds local charities to donate a portion of its proceeds to and also has a beautiful prayer wall. Make sure you stop by and write your own prayer to place on the prayer wall. There's something freeing about it.

11

Café 11 is one of the coolest beachside eateries in St. Augustine. This place has it all; breakfast, lunch and dinner menus, vegan options, smoothies, coffee, desserts to die for, a pet friendly patio and free wifi. Plus, it's across the street from the beach!

The food is fantastic, with a fresh menu full of original dishes you won't find anywhere else. The locally owned and run establishment has a great craft beer happy hour, and is famous for its weekend brunch and live music. The eclectic beach bar has hosted some astonishing musical talent. Make sure to check the website for upcoming shows. If you're lucky enough to be in town during a show at Café 11, you are lucky indeed!

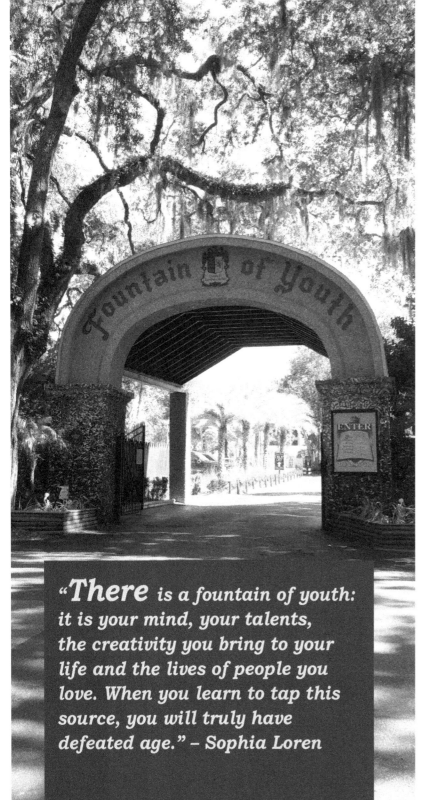

The Fountain of Youth Archeological Park is a well of information. Find out about the original settlers of St. Augustine, tour historical replicas and learn about the incredible history that started the oldest town in the United States. On your way to the Fountain of Youth, make sure you enjoy the picturesque Florida live oaks lining Magnolia Street. It's so pretty they say even Forrest Gump had to see it.

*"**There** is a fountain of youth: it is your mind, your talents, the creativity you bring to your life and the lives of people you love. When you learn to tap this source, you will truly have defeated age." – Sophia Loren*

#83 OBSERVE

"To acquire knowledge, one must study; but to acquire wisdom,

one must observe." – Marilyn vos Savant

There are so many places to take a moment to observe the eclectic surroundings of

St. Augustine. Enjoy the peace and create your own stories about what you see.

Notes: what do you see, hear, think, etc.

A small corner of Europe in St. Augustine.

Gaufre's & Goods is a hidden gem indeed. They have two locations, a cafe on Avilés Street and just around the corner on Charlotte Street, you'll find their Greek/Polish restaurant. Family owned and operated for over 10 years, this restaurant is the epitome of cultural flavor that makes dining in St. Augustine such a treat. Make sure you talk to the owners who always have beautiful words to share. Their love of cooking is evident in each dish they prepare.

LOCAL TIP

Try the pierogies with sauerkraut, bacon and onion.

ONE-OF-A-KIND
HIDDEN
GEM ST. AUGUSTINE FLORIDA
99 EPIC

"Let your light shine." – Matthew 5:16

Night of Lights is one of the most EPIC holiday light displays you'll ever see. From late November to early February the city lights up the night with more than 3 million glittering white lights. The tradition started nearly 500 years ago, marking the beginning of the holiday season with a single white candle glowing in a window of each home when St. Augustine served as the capital of Spanish La Florida. It continues today celebrating the city's grand style.

LOCAL TIP

View the lights by horse and carriage and bring your own thermos of hot cocoa.

eXplore

X Scavenger Hunts

are a fun way to entertain yourself while exploring the city. You can go on your own, at a leisurely pace or invite friends and compete with each other to cross tasks off your list. It's especially fun to follow a map through the winding streets of St. Augustine. It's easy to get lost in the allure of the old town and pretend you're on your own EPIC treasure hunt.

"It feels so good to be lost in the right direction."

"A SINGLE SUNBEAM IS ENOUGH TO DRIVE AWAY MANY SHADOWS"

ST. FRANCIS OF ASSISI

Soak up the sunshine while you're in St. Augustine.
It can do wondrous things for your soul.

"There's a whole wild world out there waiting to be explored."

The St. Augustine Alligator Farm Zoological Park is a one-of-a-kind experience. Open 365 days a year, it offers fun for all ages – rare wildlife exhibits, educational shows and even a zipline!

#89 SEE

"WHERE FLOWERS BLOOM, SO DOES HOPE." – LADY BIRD JOHNSON

St. Augustine is home to many garden enthusiasts. A walk through the residential streets downtown is like a stroll through a secret garden. Snap photos of the beautiful gardens and window boxes that adorn the historic downtown.

Check out the garden club of St. Augustine when you're in tow to find out about events.

"ENJOY THE UNEXPECTED JOURNEY LIFE HAS MAPPED OUT FOR YOU."
– C. BENJAMIN

St Augustine is a great place to people watch. Find a comfy spot and watch the world evolve around you. It's fun to ponder where everyone has come from, what they've seen and where they're going. Enjoy the wonders of the world that bring us to a certain place.

"Life is short, eat dessert first."

Indulging your sweet tooth is easy to do in St. Augustine. They take La Dolce Vida seriously. Here's a list of some of our favorite places to get a sugar high.

Bunnery Bakery & Café
Claude's Chocolate
Crème de la Cocoa @ DOS
Juniper Market
Kilwin's Chocolate
Luli's Cupcakes
Whetstone Chocolate

LOCAL TIP

Swing by Claude's Chocolate to try some of their many flavors of Truffles & Bon Bons.

Dessert

"The light shall guide you home."

The St. Augustine Lighthouse is a great place to discover the history of the nation's oldest port. It's the oldest surviving brick structure in St. Augustine.

Take a tour and climb the 219 steps for a stunning view of the first coast. The Lighthouse is dedicated to education and preservation. Check out its archeology projects and maritime museum.

"THERE'S POWER IN LOOKING SILLY AND NOT CARING THAT YOU DO."

- AMY POEHLER

An old time photo is a great way to capture the historic charm of the nation's oldest city. Plus, what a fun memory!

"Every new friend is a new adventure...
the start of more memories."
– Patrick Lindsay

Make a new friend while you're in town.

Perhaps they crossed your path for a reason.

Have them sign here.

Friend

"Be your own kind of beautiful.

The Casa Monica Hotel was originally erected in 1888 and is part of the National Trust of Historic Hotels. This building has been fully renovated and is now part of the Kessler Collection of Hotels. Everything about the Casa Monica drips luxury. Walk through the gorgeous lobby and marvel at the frescos, fountains and chandeliers.

LOCAL TIP

Enjoy a drink in the lounge to experience the Casa Monica's ambiance.

CASA MONICA

"MEMORIES ARE TIMELESS TREASURES OF THE HEART."

Pick up a souvenir that captures a memory you made here. It can be as simple as a seashell. Just find something that can carry a happy memory of this trip with you.

"The voyage of discovery is not in seeking new landscapes but in having new eyes." - Marcel Proust

The Colonial Quarter is where history comes alive! Discover the extensive history of St. Augustine through interactive tours, reenactments, exhibits and colonial dining experiences.

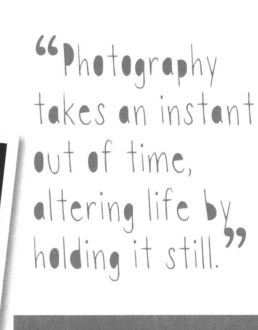

"Photography takes an instant out of time, altering life by holding it still."

- Dorothea Lange

Take artistic photos of your visit to St. Augustine. Capture the beauty you see forever.

"We must take adventures in order to know where we truly belong."

Make a list of what you want to do on your next visit

How many epic things did you do out of our 99? - Share the number with us on Social Media.

*"The best things in life
are the people we love,
the places we've been and
the memories we've made
along the way."*

People always say, "I'll do it when I have time."
That's the crazy thing about life, we never know how much time we have.
Make the time to be Epic now.

EPIC INDEX

EPIC EATS

Downtown St. Augustine

A1A Ale Works	Gaufre's & Goods
Barley Republic	Gourmet Hut
Blue Hen	Harry's Seafood
Bull & Crown	Hazel's Hotdogs
Café Alcazar	Hot Shots
Casa Maya	Ice Plant
Catch 27	Meehan's
Cellar 6	Michael's Tasting Room
Collage	Mojo BBQ
Columbia	Nonna's Trattoria
Crave	O.C. Whites
Creekside	Old City House Inn
Flavors Eatery	Raintree
The Floridian	Schmagle's Bagels

St. Augustine Beach

Beachcomber	Osteen's
Café 11	Ripe
Conch House	Salt Life
Coquina Beach Club	Stir it Up
Mango Mango's	Zaharias
Oasis	

EPIC TACOS

(we really like tacos so they get a whole section)

Burrito Works Taco Shop
Mojo's Tacos
Nalu's Tropical Takeout

EPIC DRINKS

Coffee
Casa Monica Hotel – Starbucks
Cafe Dolce
City Coffee
City Perk
Crucial Coffee
DOS Coffee
Hot Shots
Juniper Market
Kookaburra

Cocktails
Cellar 6
Dos Gatos
Ice Plant
Mojo BBQ
Oddbirds
Tini Martini Bar

Craft Beer
A1A Ale Works
Café 11
Henley's Seafood
Hoptinger
JP Henley's
Mellow Mushroom
Rendezvous
Social Lounge

Wine
Carrera Wine Cellar
Cellar 6
Centro
Columbia
Gifted Cork
Gourmet Hut
Michael's Tasting Room
Monk's Vineyard
Old City House Inn
San Sebastian Winery
Sangria's

Epic Sweets
(Satisfy your sweet tooth)
Bunnery Bakery & Café
Claude's Chocolate
Crème de la Cocoa @ DOS
Hyppo Popsicles
Hot Shots
Juniper Market
Kilwin's Chocolate
Luli's Cupcakes
Whetstone Chocolate

Epic Tunes
(Catch some live music)
Café 11
Harry's Seafood
Mi Casa
Mill Top Tavern
Music at the Pier
No Name Bar
O.C. White's
Rooftop Winery
Sangria's Piano & Jazz Bar
St. Augustine Amphitheater

Epic Sites
(Must see landmarks)
Anastasia State Park
Bridge of Lions
Castillo de San Marcos
Fountain of Youth
Historic Lincolnville
Historic Old Town
St. Augustine Beach
St. Augustine Lighthouse
St. George Street
The Old Jail

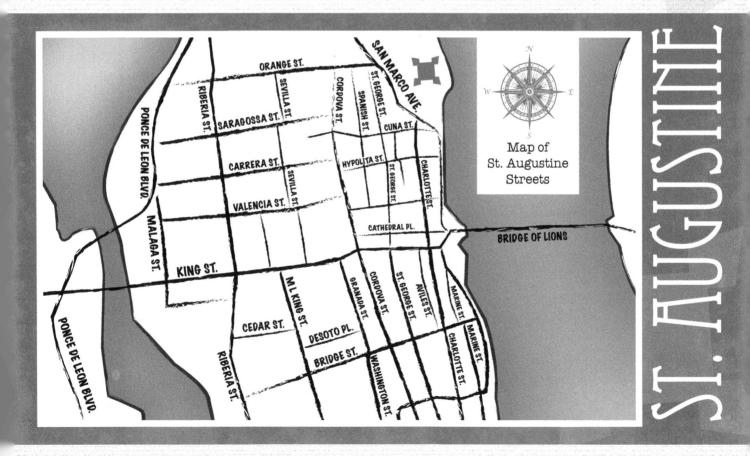

Map of St. Augustine Streets

ST. AUGUSTINE

ABOUT THE AUTHORS

Christina and Philip Benjamin are the author and designer team behind the 99 Epic series. None of the places or people they include in 99 Epic have asked them to do so. They simply had EPIC experiences and wanted to share them with readers so they can form their own EPIC memories.

The Benjamin's try to live life to the fullest and make even the smallest moments EPIC ones. They strive to focus their energy in positive ways, bringing hope, love, humor and optimism with them on their journey through life.

Christina Benjamin is a best-selling author. She's followed her heart's passion by turning writing into a full time career. You can find most of her award-winning work on Amazon.com. To find out what she's up to next check out her website. www.christinabenjaminauthor.com

Philip Benjamin is a graphic designer and founder of Benjamin Design, a design company that specializes in logos, print media and book cover design.

Together they've used their expertise to create Crown Atlantic Publishing, an independent publishing company that puts out work they feel passionate about. "We enjoy being able to work together on projects we love. Seeing a concept or idea blossom into reality is incredibly rewarding." – Christina Benjamin.

THANK YOU

for taking the time to read
99 Epic Things To Do - St. Augustine.
We are currently working on other
cities so stay tuned for more
EPIC locations to visit.

We hope you enjoyed reading this book as much as we enjoyed putting
it together. If you have time please leave a review online.
We'd love to hear about your trip so don't forget to share your
photos and comments with us on our social media sites.

FACEBOOK.COM/99EPIC   TWITTER.COM/99EPIC_TRAVEL   INSTAGRAM.COM/99EPIC